# Meditations of a Global Citizen

# Meditations of a Global Citizen

40 Reflective Quotes to Help You Live More Purposefully, Shift Your Thinking and Unleash Your Inner Humanitarian

Jordyn Hawkins-Rippie

Copyright © 2024 Jordyn Hawkins-Rippie

**All rights reserved.**

No part of this book may be reproduced, or stored in a retrieval system, or transmitted in any form or by any means, electronic, mechanical, photocopying, recording, or otherwise, without express written permission of the publisher.

ISBN: 979-8334873292

# Dedication

To the human collective, with love. May you unabashedly continue to pursue the highest, first-rate version of yourself with goodwill, authenticity and humanitarianism - the future of our world depends upon it.

# TABLE OF CONTENTS

| | |
|---|---|
| Author's Note | 8 |
| Introduction | 10 |
| On Discovering Your Purpose | 13 |
| On Shifting Your Mindset | 50 |
| On Unleashing Your Inner Humanitarian | 98 |

# Author's Note

If you are currently reading this - no matter where you may be located, what conditions you may be in and when you may be reading this - you're still operating with the most precious and consequential gift in the world: life. As a human collective, we all have the luxury of partaking in this beautiful gift of life, yet circumstance either aids and enhances or diminishes and destroys this gift that we've been given. There are those among us who live in overwhelming abundance, having the freedom to live life on the terms that they set before themselves, and then there are those among us who struggle tirelessly moment after moment with insurmountable battles to realize even an iota of what life has to offer them. Despite these differences, as a collective, both groups - regardless of race, ethnicity, age, ability, education level and gender - still face challenges in discovering purpose and the why for their life still remains somewhat of an elusive concept for them to grasp.

The great element about discovering purpose and elevating oneself is that it does not discriminate and is wildly transformational. Discovering purpose deters the well-heeled businessperson who has, by all accounts and measures, been wildly successful from spiraling out of control and leaving friends and loved ones to painfully wonder what could have caused them to end their life. Discovering purpose enables the most downtrodden among us in spirit to regain a vitality in their soul by using their gifts to create a new life trajectory not only for their immediate family, but also their entire community.

No matter where you fall along the spectrum of life and circumstance, know that changing your mindset, finding purpose and unleashing the humanitarian spirit within you is well within your reach and that the world has no other choice but to bow before you as you selflessly give unto it that for which you have been called.

As you exist right here and right now, a treasure trove of gold and diamonds resides within your spirit and it is my mission to help you extract these riches to elevate your life, purpose and impact on this world. Before journeying through these pages, I want you to make this promise to yourself: no matter how many obstacles come your way or how hard the road of your life may seem, maintain faith and expectation that you will not leave this earth before fulfilling your mission and that your steps are being ordered in the most divine way.

Jordyn Hawkins-Rippie

# Introduction

*Meditations of a Global Citizen* originated from over ten years of creating quotations on a multitude of topics that have always been near and dear to my heart. I first began sharing originally penned quotes in 2013 as I was transitioning from high school to university and I always had the intent to motivate, encourage and offer up another perspective on various topics. Although I started down the journey of encouraging others through my quotes in 2013, it wouldn't be until 2018 while serving as an English Teaching Assistant with the Fulbright U.S. Student Program in Malaysia for the year where I started creating quotes on a more consistent basis. From 2018 to now, I have created and shared quotes on social media platforms such as Facebook and Instagram to encourage the global collective towards mutual uplift in hopes that mindset shifts could be realized to alter the course of humanity as we know it. So why a reflective quote book in particular and why now?

Right now, the global collective is terribly lost and hurting. Take an honest look at the conditions around us. Social and economic strife, abject poverty and the callous treatment of humans towards each other plagues groups of people wherever we turn. People present cheerful and jovial personalities in public while secretly battling mental health issues and substance abuse in private. Individuals are desperately searching for their unique purpose for which they were called in this lifetime oftentimes to little or no avail, driving greater anxieties and frustrations in families and communities everywhere.

Institutions of governance and political leaders have eroded trust with the communities that they serve and countries operating in a spirit of cooperation towards the continuance of humanity as we know it has become increasingly harder to find. Our precious habitats are being destroyed around the world with reckless disregard and wildlife that helps to maintain ecological order is disappearing at alarming rates. We are more divided than ever before and the tapestry upon which history plays out is quickly coming apart at the seams. One need not look far to see that our world is in disarray and in serious need of guidance and healing.

My intention with this reflective quote book is for you to journey with me towards developing and enhancing your spirit and mindset positively for you to discover purpose and unleash your inner humanitarian. Yes, each and every one of you has the potential to develop a humanitarian spirit by selflessly stewarding our gifts to the world for the uplift of its people. I have structured the journal for readers as follows: each chapter will present a topic of discussion along with my original quotes, explanations, reflection questions and affirmations to encourage the incorporation of the learnings into your life. I have taken the liberty to include some of my quotes as standalone quotes without reflections to allow you to generate your own thoughts and responses to what I am communicating in the quote and encourage you to discuss your perspectives on those quotes with friends or anyone else who may be interested in them. The chapter topics are in no particular order and every chapter may not necessarily resonate or be applicable to your situation based on where you are in your own journey, so I encourage you to utilize the book in a way that works best for you and to skip around to topics in which you're most interested.

It is critical to not only meditate upon the quotes themselves, but also upon your own reflection question answers, as you may delightfully come to certain realizations and aha moments as you engage the content. Given the reflective nature of the content, I encourage readers to use a simple breathing technique as such:

- Breathe in deeply through your nose for at least three seconds
- Hold your breath for at least three seconds
- Exhale through your mouth for at least three seconds

This process should be done a few times prior to reading the quote and before journaling your response to the reflection questions. The goal in this process is to create a present mindfulness that will focus your thoughts and reflections towards truly extracting the gems you need out of the content.

It is my sincere hope that both the insights in these quotes coupled with your own answers to the reflective questions radically alter the course of your thinking and perspectives for the better and that you refer back to the content often as inspiration and encouragement in your own life journey. Let your thoughts flow freely and write in the margins, highlight quotes that resonate with you and get carried away in the thoughts you generate towards the content. Everyone will generate reflections that are personal and specific to them, but if you feel compelled, share your perspectives with another person or within a group to discuss, for you may find that someone seemingly with many differences from you on the surface may share commonality and community over something that you both believe deep within your minds and spirits. With that said, if you're ready to venture with me and countless others down a journey of transformation, let's begin.

# On Discovering Your Purpose

*Every year of life we get the chance to continue painting upon life's canvas, creating our own expressive masterpieces that contribute to the narrative of the human experience.*

Life is the most precious gift in the world. With each passing year through our actions, we build upon the brushstrokes of the previous years to continue creating our own grand masterpiece. When done with intentionality, the process of creating this work of art has the ability to transform the lives of all who gaze upon it for better or for worse. Consider this:

1. Identify two pivotal years of your life in which you witnessed a positive and negative transformation of yourself - what was your own and other people's emotional reaction to this transformation in the positive year and the negative one? How did this make you feel?

2. At this moment, is your life transforming and developing in the direction that you envisioned it and how does that make you feel? If so, what strategies have been successful in continuing in this direction and if not, what is within your control to alter the trajectory that it is on or to educate another person about the pitfalls of this trajectory?

**Affirmation:** "Each and every day, I have the opportunity to craft and shape the trajectory of my life for the better and educate others based on my own life experiences."

*There's something that you do naturally well, gives your life a deep vibrancy when engaged in doing it and touches others in a profound way that seems effortless - that's where your calling is. That's your mission on this earth.*

There are three elements to purpose - natural giftedness, alignment with spirit and edification of those around you. When all of these converge, one can accurately pinpoint that for which they have been called. In bringing forth your purpose to the world, it will never manifest itself fully if you seek to destroy those around you - it must serve as a guiding light for whatever you're engaged in doing. For example, someone may have an excellent spirit of emotional intelligence, but if they are operating to manipulate someone emotionally instead of emotionally guiding them through a tough time and edifying them, the gift will never reach its highest heights. Reflect on this:

1. What is something that you can do naturally well, gives you deep vibrancy and touches others profoundly without having been formally educated to do it? What is a space that you would thrive in only if you possessed additional formal training coupled with your already innate gifts?

2. What activities make you come alive when engaged in them and also garners overwhelmingly positive reception from others?

___

**Affirmation:** "I am divinely purposed to fulfill a special mission that only I have been called to fulfill here on this earth."

*Your authenticity flows from the well-spring of your character values.*

1. What character traits have people mostly identified you with and how do those identifications make you feel?

_____
_____
_____
_____
_____
_____
_____
_____
_____
_____
_____
_____
_____
_____
_____
_____
_____

2. Is there anything that you would alter about your current set of character values and how would you go about changing them?

_____
_____
_____
_____
_____
_____
_____
_____
_____
_____
_____
_____
_____
_____

**Affirmation:** "I am actively edifying my spirit through the adoption of positive character values that allow me to live on my own authentic terms."

*We are conditioned to compare ourselves in every way imaginable to others in nearly every aspect of daily living, but when you operate in your purpose you understand that your purpose, by nature, is not comparative, but rather distinct, uniquely crafted for fulfillment by you and you alone.*

Understand that you have a mission on this planet that you and only you can carry out - to compare your mission to another is not possible when you're operating with this knowledge, for no one mission is ever the same. In discovering purpose, you discover what you and only you alone can bring into the world, opening the doors of opportunity to help humanity as defined by that mission.

_____

_____

_____

_____

_____

**Affirmation:** "I am walking boldly in my own path and purpose."

*The reason your life path isn't prematurely revealed to you is because you'd turn back at the prospect of what you would have to endure and the transformations that you would have to undergo to become your highest self.*

Life's lessons are intended to build our resolve and give us greater insights into our place and role we play in this world, but without those lessons we lose appreciation for our strong spirits and the process of building them. We must come to fully accept that without these life events and lessons we could not grow wiser to impart wisdom to others and to heal the human collective, which is something we all have the capacity of doing with our respective life experiences. There is great value in your life experiences despite what anyone may tell you and every person has lessons and stories of lived experiences that we should all humbly embrace as a part of the tapestry of collective intelligence in the world. Consider this:

1. What life experiences, good and bad, do you think another individual would gain insightful value from your sharing of those experiences with them?

2. Think about a life defining experience you had that when going through it you didn't enjoy but look back upon gratefully on - how did this experience make you stronger and more resolute in your values and what you stand for today?

_____
_____
_____
_____
_____
_____
_____
_____
_____

**Affirmation:** "I lean confidently into all experiences that come into my life with the expectation that they will yield greater insights and edification for my overall self."

*Creative expression frees us from the multilayered facade of identity that society impresses upon us.*

Oftentimes individuals in society are forced to wear certain masks for fear of showing their true selves to everyone and this debases us of our dignity of self and everything that we stand for and represent. In any work or action that we take towards the world, we are expressing ourselves all of the time and we should always strive to express our highest, authentic selves because that is where we experience our greatest birthright of freedom. Think about this:

1. In what ways do you feel that society has impressed its value system upon your own internal one? Do you feel authentic in your expression of your value system despite this?

_____
_____
_____
_____
_____

2. Envision you expressing every element of your inner self for the rest of the world to see without judgment - what would that look like? How would this expression positively elevate those around you?

**Affirmation:** "I march confidently in authenticity, positivity and creativity without compromising who I am at my core."

*If you perceive that you will have any ounce of regret for not having pursued an opportunity when looking back over your life, by all means pursue it.*

We all want to live a full life and be able to reflect and genuinely say that we pursued everything that we wanted to pursue in our lives. However, fear coupled with a perceived lack of preparation often stops us in our tracks from pursuing that which we know could potentially catapult our lives in a radically different trajectory for the better. If we are fortunate, a missed opportunity will reappear at a later point in time, but many times the life-defining ones that are powerful enough to change the entire trajectory of our destiny only come around once for us to pursue. Reflect on this:

1. What is an opportunity that came to you but you were too afraid to take? Why were you afraid to take this opportunity and how did that make you feel?

2. Envision the type of opportunities that you would want to encounter - what can you do now to best prepare yourself if these opportunities presented themselves to you?

_____

_____

_____

_____

_____

_____

_____

**Affirmation:** "I courageously pursue opportunities that present themselves to me with a fearless spirit."

*Spend a few hours each day growing your proficiency in a space you want to become world-class in - you will have expanded significantly within the first year and be on track to owning your craft several years down the road. Expertise does not reveal itself to the swift builder, but rather the methodical and gradually progressive one.*

The path to mastery of your craft lies in continual practice upon it, day in and day out, with a focused mind that builds on the work done previously. Many seek to experience quick, short-lived wins while building, not understanding that the process of building anything may take quite some time before any type of progress is readily observed. With this in mind:

1. What is something that you have built towards that has taken a long time to realize any perceivable change and how did that make you feel?

2. What is a skill that you would like to master and why?

_____
_____
_____
_____

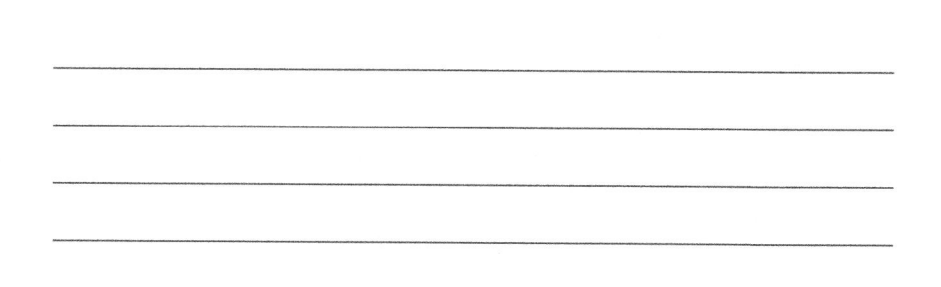

**Affirmation:** "I make progress with each and every step of action I take towards achieving my ultimate goals."

*Mine your diamonds in altering, impacting, liberating and inspiring the minds of men.*

Each of us will be called to different career paths and the beauty in discovering that path is that when we excel in whatever it is that we are called to do, it gives us an even greater platform to amplify any causes we care about to a much wider audience. We see countless examples of top athletes, entertainers and celebrities using their influence to bring awareness to certain causes and, for many, their advocacy work becomes just as or even more known than the talents that gave them the platform to begin. Whatever we do, we must aim to shift individuals' awareness and understanding of the world to sustain the future of it. Consider this:

1. In your current capacity, how do you inspire people in your sphere of influence towards becoming better versions of themselves?

2. What feelings do you seek to create in people once they have interacted with you and why? How can you be intentional about creating an environment for them to leave you feeling the way you intended?

_____
_____
_____
_____
_____
_____
_____

**Affirmation:** "I boldly transform the perspectives and minds of those around me through my platform and influence."

*Each and every person has within a spark of genius the world desperately needs and it is up to you to selflessly draw it out to edify the collective human condition.*

There exists a deep reservoir of abilities inside of you waiting to be brought forward to those around you in the world - your own personal spark along with everyone else bringing forth their respective spark helps to collectively energize the world towards overall betterment of its condition. Ask yourself this:

1. Within your relationships and friendships, what do you believe are the primary attributes you contribute to those groups for which people celebrate you?

_____
_____
_____
_____
_____

_____

_____

_____

_____

_____

_____

_____

**Affirmation:** "I faithfully steward the best attributes of myself to the world to both improve the conditions and uplift the spirits of those around me."

*Never allow worldly qualifications to determine your altitude in your life endeavors - when you operate in your gift and calling, unfettered by the opinions of anyone, the freedom you experience will naturally elevate you to spaces and unlock doors in ways unforeseen.*

Many of us endeavor to obtain further education in the form of classes, certificates and degrees because education may be required to work in certain spaces such as law and medicine or to simply enhance our overall livelihoods from an earning perspective. While obtaining further education can position one to increase their overall livelihood, the foundation upon which they are building this knowledge must be built upon the innate gifts that they possess to truly stand out and shine in an area. When we start first with discovering our innate gifts, we establish where our own abilities can take us in the world as well as any limitations of those abilities.

Supercharging our lives means habitually practicing and owning our gifts and then building upon a solid foundation of our gifts with additional training and education if necessary. Some of us will never need to enter into formal education to truly operate at the highest level of our gifts while others of us will need to complement our gifts with such education, but the idea is that regardless of where you fall along the spectrum, both start with the foundational innate gifts that we possess. Reflect on this:

1. What are some innate qualities - independent of any educational journey - that you naturally seem to possess and do you believe you can operate fully in them without additional training and education?

_____
_____
_____
_____
_____
_____

2. In your education journey, do you feel that your experiences valued building upon the innate gifts and skills that you already possessed and how does that make you feel?

**Affirmation**: "I build my foundation upon my innate gifts and talents to optimize the impact that I have in the world."

*In the end, if what gives you meaning and purpose isn't set ablaze through your life's work, is it worth the endeavor?*

Decisions are a quintessential part of this life and they have the ability to shape the course of our lives for the better or for the worse. Rarely do we evaluate a decision professionally with what we want our ultimate legacy to be in mind, but we must do so if we wish to chart the course of our lives in a way that brings us in alignment with that for which we are called and purposed. Consider this:

1. Evaluate the work with which you are currently involved professionally or personally - is this work that resonates with your soul on a deep level and why?

_____
_____
_____

2. What activities do you naturally do well in that creates a vibrancy within your soul?

3. Imagine you are on your deathbed - what endeavors do you perceive that you would have regretted not pursuing if you had the opportunity to pursue them?

___

**Affirmation**: "I wholeheartedly pursue experiences that enliven my spirit and give meaning to my existence."

*Steward your gifts and talents humbly and confidently, reassured in the calling on your life.*

The gifts that we have been naturally given at birth are unique and special to us and us alone. We recognize that anyone else could have been blessed with what we have, but the gifts were given to us with a reason: that we never take them for granted and use them to empower those around us in the world. It pays to demonstrate humility to show people your healthy spirit and confidence that you and only you can bring forth your gifts to the world.

_____

_____

_____

_____

_____

_____

_____

_____

_____

_____

**Affirmation:** "I rest assured that the calling on my life will be fulfilled."

# On Shifting Your Mindset

*Every encounter with an individual is another chance to substantively play a part of the edification and mindset shift of that individual so that they, in turn, can reciprocally do the same for others in their spheres of influence.*

Each and every one of us has the potential to direct the energy that we carry towards positively uplifting other members of the global collective. We make the choice to operate in either constructive and loving energy, building up those around us, or destructive and unloving energy, tearing down others of those around us. There is no neutrality with the energy we choose to demonstrate towards others. Consider this:

1. Look at the people in your immediate sphere of influence - has the energy you put out created the conditions for those people to grow and develop into their best selves or has it cut them down and caused them to stagnate in their growth and development?

_____
_____
_____
_____
_____
_____
_____
_____
_____
_____

2. Identify ways in which you can redirect any destructive energy towards turning it into constructive and uplifting energy - what are your strategies and how do you want people to feel about the energy that you're giving them?

**Affirmation:** "I radiate and exude a powerful spirit of positivity in all of my interactions while encouraging others towards their best selves."

*Every once and awhile, step away from the cacophony of societal expectations thrust upon you by your immediate and broader surroundings and enter into the world of inner thought to critically assess and build your own intuitive interpretations of the external world.*

The media has dominated society's thoughts, ways of living and what we place value and importance upon in our world since its inception. Since the majority of individuals in society consume and utilize similar media sources and content, echo chambers are often created in which original, independent thought is feared, shunned and castigated. Stepping away from the mainstream fray and being alone to your own thoughts and self to truly begin to understand our world, how you want to engage with it and what you personally value is something that can be perplexing to many; in that private space, no one is telling you what you what you want to hear about the world and validate your opinions, thoughts or agree with you for the sake of agreement. You must face yourself as you exist and are often forced to confront your beliefs, decisions and circumstances with raw honesty and introspection, which is never an easy thing. However in this place of uncomfortability and vulnerability, you begin to understand parts of yourself that you would have never fully understood surrounded by constant opinions and perspectives bombarding your mind. These conditions are the grounds for deep transformation within yourself ultimately. Think about this:

1. When was the last time that you spent genuine quality time alone without any distractions? How did it feel to have that time to yourself and what did you learn about yourself, your motivations and your desires in that space and time?

_____

_____

_____

_____

_____

2. Do you currently have the ability to spend a significant amount of time alone in reflection on a consistent basis when issues and problems arise? How can you be more intentional about creating the conditions around space and time to honor the nurturing of your spirit and reflect?

**Affirmation:** "I provide myself ample time and space to form my own values, perspectives and conclusions independent of any external perspectives the world presents me."

*Cultivating an ethos of humility and outstanding service in prospective and current client interactions is quintessential to the success of winning and maintaining business in client-facing professions; whether it's a senior-level director in the financial services, a partner in the legal space or other senior-level decision maker in other client-facing spaces, he or she realizes the technical acumen is only buoyed by exhibiting a high level of emotional intelligence and genuine relatability.*

Everyone is involved in the business of people at the end of the day. No matter what professional field you enter into, people will ultimately be the direct or indirect recipient of some service, product or information.

Humanizing the element of our business while placing those people being served at the focal point creates the conditions for organizations of all types and sizes to have the impact they truly seek while doing the greatest good for all who are involved. Reflect on this:

1. In organizations that you have been or currently are associated with, what is the philosophy and overall ethos, if any, as it regards the people that are being served and do you feel that those organizations have been authentic and true to themselves in this regard? How does this make you feel?

_____
_____
_____
_____
_____
_____
_____
_____

2. How have you personally demonstrated technical expertise alongside emotional and cultural empathy in the personal and professional ecosystems in which you operate?

_____
_____
_____
_____
_____
_____
_____
_____

3. How can you better facilitate organizational alignment with what you seek to accomplish and that with which you actually accomplish for the intended recipients of your personal or professional activities? What lasting impressions do you seek to leave in the minds of the people you're serving?

_____
_____
_____

_____
_____
_____
_____
_____
_____
_____
_____

**Affirmation:** "I empathetically humanize my interactions with others while providing outstanding service to those whom I serve to create an ethical and people-focused environment in which I conduct my work and activities."

*Once you allow another individual to craft your uniquely defined life narrative, you relinquish your ability to live life on your own authentic terms.*

The lives we decide to live can only be lived out by us and us alone. Yet, the external forces of societal pressures and the internal feelings of not measuring up to arbitrary standards we have imposed upon ourselves cause us to take on lives we may have never intended. Remove any masks of identity that cloud your mental, spiritual and physical well-being and authenticity and simply live a life beholden to your innermost aligned self. The most powerful thing you can do for your authenticity is to simply live in such a way that is true to who you are at your core to allow the best nourishment for your soul. Consider this:

1. Do you feel that anyone has ever created a false narrative around your identity and what you stand for in your life? If so, how did it make you feel and how did you counter the narrative?

_____
_____
_____
_____
_____
_____
_____
_____
_____
_____

2. How have you protected your narrative from being changed and kept the authenticity of your identity and that for which you stand?

**Affirmation:** " I stand boldly and aligned on my identity, life experiences and narratives while living life in my own authentic way."

*Seemingly disparate concepts and ways of thinking almost always present room for commonalities to be discovered and existing paradigms to be shifted - nothing is ever completely foreign to another.*



In navigating the world of ideologies, beliefs and behaviors, much of the focus is placed upon the differences that exist between or among these differences with only a casual attempt at seeking to discover areas where they converge. When these similarities are fleshed out, it allows greater mutual understanding in a space and, in some cases, brings individuals to agreement on things previously considered a point of disagreement. We ultimately strengthen our overall understanding of something in fully knowing where the differences and similarities exist. Think about this:

1. How does this quote make you feel about the value of differing perspectives and your willingness to seek commonalities amidst differences?

_____
_____
_____
_____
_____
_____
_____
_____
_____
_____

2. How are you actively advocating for and showing up in the ecosystems you occupy to serve as a bridge builder for differing concepts, people and ways of doing things?

**Affirmation:** "I seek to bridgebuild and navigate differences in my environment with understanding and empathy."

*The military-industrial complex continues to ramp up propaganda to cover its own egregious, imperialistic missteps through overwhelmingly biased channels of information - seek knowledge from independent sources who have not cozied up to and are not directly funded by corporatists.*

1. How do you feel overall about the military funding and spending in your country and what effect does this have on the outlook of other countries towards yours?

_____
_____
_____
_____
_____
_____
_____
_____

2. What are your thoughts on the role of money and media within politics and what are your thoughts on redirecting power back into the hands of the constituents?

**Affirmation:** "I discern the media narratives that I consume and diversify the sources that I consume to offer an even greater perspective on world issues."

*Embrace the faith building process that accompanies being in the midst of uncertainty.*

Faith is a muscle and, like a muscle, unless we want it to atrophy, we must exercise it on a continuous basis. We build resolve and strength when we cannot always see what lies ahead on our journey and with each triumphant step forward we continue to build even greater strength to conquer greater things in our lives. We should welcome the opportunity to rise to the occasion and become stronger in our area of faith, for we become a fortress of emotional and mental fortitude that will remain standing despite all odds. Consider this:

1. Have you ever had to trust something or someone without knowing all of the details about how to proceed forward? How did it make you feel in the moment and why do you think it made you feel that way?

2. What strategies can you creatively envision to help you navigate those moments where you do not have clarity and do not know how to proceed forward?

_____

_____

_____

_____

**Affirmation**: "I lean into uncertainty in the circumstances where I don't have the complete picture and details and trust that everything is working in my favor."

*You are evolving - those things, people and places which no longer serve to edify you will fade away and you will experience an abundance of living life from an elevated perspective.*

As we go through life, one of the hardest internal acknowledgements to make to ourselves is realizing that our connection and association to certain people, places or things actually stymies our overall progress. In the process of maturing spiritually, emotionally, mentally and physically, we naturally set boundaries with associations that are familiar because we understand the conditions that must be created to maintain the peace and serenity that comes from that growth. Entering into new levels of our life dictates that we assess who or what can come with us to those levels and the old cannot occupy space with the new. Reflect on this:

1. What people, things and circumstances personally affect your joy, happiness and well-being in your life? If something no longer serves you, why does it no longer serve you and how do you feel about moving forward from it?

_____
_____
_____
_____
_____
_____
_____
_____
_____
_____
_____

**Affirmation:** "I am intentional about occupying and creating space for people and conditions that nourish my spirit and overall well-being."

*Counterculture is what we strive toward when the culture has become bereft of spiritual edification and moral clarity - you have a choice: run with crowd, constantly chasing ever-fleeting concepts of impact and meaning or brace the world and live your truth to organically create the environment for these concepts to naturally attract to your work. The grand scale impact you seek will not be found in going with the masses - world changers go against entire systems of thinking and methodologies of doing things. It's never too late to alter and course correct - on which side of history will you be remembered?*

_____
_____
_____
_____
_____
_____
_____

*The true spiritual degradation of a people perpetuates itself through willful avoidance of that which is hard truth - true freedom comes at a cost and many are not willing to die to their ignorance to evolve.*

Oftentimes we remain mired in the same cycles and patterns that negatively affect us because in the depths of our minds and souls exist deeply uncomfortable truths about ourselves that we can't bear to face in our current conditions. Because we avoid these truths, they germinate, grow and take hold of our decision making process and cloud our ability to think and act soundly in our lives. This process becomes so strong that we continue to act against our own best self interest even when confronted on these truths, leading to chaos and destruction of our being. It is only when we face these unpleasant pieces of our identity and commit to purging ourselves of associated behaviors and thoughts that we can begin to heal, die to our old selves and truly evolve. Consider this:

1. Are there hard truths about yourself, someone else or something where you had to accept these truths for what they are and how did that make you feel?

___

2. What are ways in which you can personally act to confront hard truths about people, places and circumstances in your life to help you evolve as an individual?

___

**Affirmation**: "I wholeheartedly embrace the transformative nature of confronting deep-seated and tough truths to evolve to my highest self."

*Imagine primary and secondary educators serving in a more consultative capacity as "purpose coaches" seeking to center their pedagogy around unlocking students' innate gifts. Evaluative standards are shifted from excelling in a wide range of subjects towards honing their gifts - learning becomes more immersive and engaging, in turn producing better educational outcomes.*

*Influence, social status, money and power can both liberate and bind - most perceive liberation when really it is bondage disguised as freedom.*

Everything comes at a price - we must determine whether or not we are willing to pay the price associated with whatever it may be that we're seeking. We can readily identify examples of individuals who seem to have most or all of these things in abundance, yet still somehow remain empty, unsatisfied and in some cases in a worse state of being prior to when they started pursuing these things. Influence, social status, money and power are simply amplifiers for the spirit you carry inside of you prior to encountering any of these elements. You may have a spirit of generosity and when you come into more money, that spirit of generosity will be amplified for even greater charity and contribution. Conversely, if you have a spirit of stinginess and come into money, that spirit will be amplified as well, causing you to withhold even more than you already do. With this:

1. How have you used your influence, social status, money or power to positively enhance and uplift the lives of those around you? How have you used these same elements to destroy or control the lives of the people around you, if at all, and how does that make you feel?

_____
_____
_____
_____
_____
_____
_____
_____
_____

2. What sacrifices did you have to make to attain your current level of influence, money, wealth and social status? Were your sacrifices worth what you gained in your estimation and did it make you feel the way you imagined it would prior to arriving to that point?

3. If you could pursue any degree of these four things over again, would you change anything in your strategy towards attaining them and why?

**Affirmation**: "I am using my money, status, influence and power to collectively uplift and steward goodness to those around me. I will not compromise any elements of my core beliefs, values and identity to attain any of these things."

*The simple, authentic and truly free life is the ultimate goal - only a few will ever truly experience this level of boundless living.*

If we're honest with ourselves, we will be able to acknowledge that a lot of what we seek materially either brings little or short-lived satisfaction to our lives and in some cases greater complication to our situations. We should enjoy the material things this world has to offer us, especially if we've worked hard for them, but we have to ensure that we do not make idols of these materials either. One can point to situations where an individual perceived that something such as a nicer car, increase in compensation, new house or brand name clothing would enhance someone's livelihood, only to discover that they still have that emptiness within them after the immediate feeling of purchasing something new wears off. Reflect on this:

1. What does true freedom look like for you in your life and why?

___

2. Have you ever purchased something out of emptiness in hopes that it would fill a void inside of you? How did it make you feel after the feeling of purchasing something new wore off?

___

3. With your current lifestyle, is there anything that you own or any activities that you engage in that you feel costs you your authenticity?

**Affirmation**: "I am living blissfully free of anyone's expectations of me and I seek abundance and meaning in living my life boldly and authentically."

*It's critically important to understand - at a fundamental level - the traditions, beliefs and practices of world religions, especially as we become more domestically and globally interdependent with others in nearly all spaces.*

1. Reflect on your knowledge of other spiritual and religious systems different from yours and examples of how understanding another's spiritual or religious system can aid in creating more understanding in the world.

**Affirmation**: "I respectfully engage with those who believe differently than I and seek to find the universal commonalities that bind me to the larger human collective."

*A country's strength results from its collective ability to celebrate the ever-present diversity in all its forms that exists all while being inspired toward the enduring principles that unify its conscience towards the greater good.*

Diversity, as it exists, encompasses not just different races and ethnicities - we must be fully aware of all forms of identity upon which something is composed. Age, ability, socioeconomic status, gender, race, ethnicity, sexual orientation, religion - peer a bit more closely into any community and, by these standards, you will come to realize that nearly every community in which we operate is diverse to some extent in a multitude of ways. Like a well-oiled military unit, a country seeking to realize its greatest potential must intimately know the abilities of the people with which it engages and make the necessary alignments in order to match appropriate skill sets and abilities to achieve optimal performance. With this:

1. Think about the environments, personally and professionally, in which you operate - what types of diversity are present? Which types of diversity are not present? How does this make you feel?

_____
_____
_____
_____
_____
_____
_____
_____
_____

2. Candidly, what elements of diversity, if any, are you uncomfortable with in your personal and professional life?

_____
_____
_____
_____

3. In what ways can you aid in becoming a better advocate for various forms of diversity without compromising who you are and what you fundamentally believe?

_____
_____
_____
_____
_____
_____
_____
_____
_____
_____
_____
_____

**Affirmation:** "I celebrate the rich diversity of the human tapestry in its various forms around me and believe that its presence makes us stronger towards understanding one another."

*Ambition, as with many things, manifests itself dually in one's life: when exercised healthily, it can elevate both one's life work and align one to the right people and circumstances and when exercised unhealthily can lead to the swift destruction of one's work and isolation of potential champions of the work and causes one supports.*

It is within our nature to continually strive to improve our current condition and station in life. We understand that generally improving our lives socially, economically, spiritually and otherwise can bring about a more vibrant livelihood and existence, but we must always consider the cost that it takes to create our ideal conditions. In striving towards building the life of our dreams, we must consistently assess and reassess how we are directing our energy towards improving our condition. Think about this:

This is where we discover whether or not our striving collectively helps those around us or if it destroys both our spirit and the spirit of those around us in the process.

1. In the pursuit of your goals, has your striving brought people closer to your mission for the betterment of their lives or has it alienated people from your mission to their detriment?

2. Envision the ecosystem in which you are striving for your goals - has your presence and specific role within that ecosystem uplifted its members and their morale or alienated its members and eroded their morale?

_____
_____
_____
_____
_____
_____
_____
_____
_____
_____

3. In what ways can you positively embolden the members of the ecosystem in which you operate to drive greater morale and appreciation of the diversity of skill and talent present within the ecosystem?

**Affirmation:** "I continually strive to achieve my goals in a healthy, uplifting way that empowers and inspires those around me while impacting the world."

# On Unleashing Your Inner Humanitarian

*One of the greatest gifts you can leave the world with is having pursued the edification of humanity with a selfless spirit - a spirit that continually seeks not only to look solely towards one's condition as the indicator for how well things are, but rather outwardly upon society to gauge conditions improving as a result of one's hopeful efforts to better it.*

By the time you leave this world, you will have either built up humanity for the better or torn it down with that with which you have been given. This extends beyond friends, family and others close to you - your spirit should be consistent across the board and within your scope of influence. If you look out and see that the conditions and circumstances of those around you have been enhanced, it will be a life well lived. Waste no opportunity and leave it all on the line to build up those around you for the better. Consider this:

1. Are you building the collective of humanity up within your sphere of influence and scope of the work in which you are engaged? How does what you're building toward make you feel?

_____
_____
_____
_____
_____
_____
_____
_____
_____
_____

2. What legacy do you want to leave to your family and the world when you are gone and how do you want to be remembered? What does achieving this legacy look like to you?

**Affirmation**: " I am continually using my position, influence and gifts to elevate the conditions of those around me in society."

*A writer's critique of society and its norms opens up and invites the reader to journey down a path of lost understanding and reconciliation of the eternal human values that have molded the very societies we continually extol.*

*The material, tangible things are not what have the most lasting implications; rather, the bevy of human emotions that run the gamut of genuine sympathy to total abjection has the most profound and direct effect on our quality of living. To direct even the slightest bit of emotion toward another individual can alter their personal paradigms, either for the better or worse. Consider how powerful our emotions are in terms of affecting other people around us: it's the one priceless asset we have at our disposal to make a significant change in another person's life. Let's passionately exude understanding, compassionate emotions towards others because, in the end, all of us simply want to be understood and valued.*

Each of us is experiencing life together at the same time and we have enough individual energy to direct toward another person to either elevate or diminish their spirit. The wonderful realization is that it costs nothing to share our joyful energy with others.

1. How have you shown up for someone in your life in a compassionate and empathetic way and how did it make them feel?

_____
_____
_____
_____
_____
_____
_____
_____
_____
_____
_____
_____

2. Do you feel good with how you regulate your emotional thermostat in your interactions with others? In what ways can you positively enhance your emotional thermostat in dealing with others?

___

**Affirmation**: " I am leading with empathy and love in my interactions with others and possess profound power to positively enhance the lives of those around me."

*International education serves to piece together the seemingly complex narrative of the depth and breadth of the human experience.*

The human collective is a tapestry of people from different places, time periods, backgrounds, experiences and identities - an education that seeks to understand this collective and solve some of the most pressing issues facing our world today must be global in nature. Reflect on this:

1. In your education journey, has an emphasis on developing a global outlook been pushed as something that you should learn to do and value?

_____
_____
_____
_____
_____

_____
_____
_____
_____

2. Has your perspective on something ever shifted after engaging with someone from another culture, background or nation? How did that shift make you feel after it happened?

_____
_____
_____
_____
_____
_____
_____

**Affirmation**: "I intentionally seek educational experiences that grow my experience and knowledge of the world around me."

*A genuine, enthusiastic willingness to engage other individuals with whom we share great differences allows us to better grasp the totality of human thought and experience.*

Many of us relegate ourselves to personal, professional and social networks that are strikingly homogenous because that's what is most comfortable and familiar to us. In order to be able to navigate effectively in today's world, however, we have to be willing to engage others who think and act differently than ourselves and be open to new experiences that will grow us positively. Consider this:

1. When was the last time that you sought out to connect with someone who identified differently than you for an activity or event? How did you feel when you connected with this individual?

2. Do you feel as though you practice genuinely inclusive ways of exploring other people's perspectives on things and what scares you most about engaging people different than you?

**Affirmation:** "I celebrate the present diversity I'm surrounded by and respect everyone's right to their beliefs and ways of being."

*I seek to inspire an entire generation to genuinely collaborate across the multifaceted spectrum of identities to create sustainable change across global communities.*

1. When was the last time that you collaborated with someone who identified differently from you along racial, socioeconomic, age, ability, gender and religious lines? How did that experience make you feel and what hesitations did you feel inside as you participated in this collaboration?

_____
_____
_____
_____
_____
_____
_____
_____
_____
_____
_____

2. What elements of the collaboration pleasantly surprised you, if any, and what lessons did you learn from that collaboration regarding vulnerability, trust and communication to achieve the desired outcome you all were seeking?

_____
_____
_____
_____
_____
_____
_____
_____
_____

**Affirmation:** "I am using my unique gifts and talents to further the aim of creating sustainable environments and change around me."

*Today's emerging leaders must be readily willing to embrace differing ideologies and strive for mutual understanding on all fronts to elevate the collective aim of global prosperity.*

We are operating in an increasingly globalized world that continues to erode the multitude of barriers put up to prevent us from collaborating and achieving real change. The most effective leaders of tomorrow will be able to understand the nature and nuances of this shift, galvanizing people from all walks of life around various causes and initiatives. In understanding this:

1. Identify a situation where someone presented a differing viewpoint from yours - how did you initially react to this? If allowed, did you give agency to this viewpoint for it to be genuinely considered?

2. How often have you exposed yourself to or actively learned from opposing ideologies to the ones that you hold? What commonalities and differences did you observe and why do you feel the way you do about both the commonalities and differences?

**Affirmation:** "I am actively creating the conditions for positive collaboration and clear understanding in the atmospheres I occupy."

*Individuals who engage in international exchange experiences actively and collectively play a significant role in shaping the narratives surrounding their countries - they bring unique, varied life experiences and backgrounds with them from which others can learn.*

We are operating in an increasingly globalized world that continues to erode the multitude of barriers put up to prevent us from collaborating and achieving real change. The most effective leaders of tomorrow will be able to understand the nature and nuances of this shift, galvanizing people from all walks of life around various causes and initiatives. In understanding this:

1. If you have traveled abroad, in what ways do you believe your identity and life experiences from your perspective shaped both how you were perceived and your overall experience? If not, in what ways do you believe your identity

and life experiences from your perspective shaped communities different from yours in your country?

_____

_____

_____

_____

_____

_____

_____

_____

_____

_____

_____

_____

_____

2. In your interactions with the citizens of countries you have visited or individuals of different communities that you have engaged with, which elements of your culture and identity have generated the most conversation and positive reception?

**Affirmation:** "The identity, experiences and narratives that I carry with me across the world is wonderfully unique and incredibly special to those that I engage with in my travels."

*Our world has become too interdependent to approach solutions to the problems that persist in our global community through a singularly focused lens - a multifaceted approach must be interdisciplinary and comparative in nature, considering the bevy of perspectives to buoy the collective.*

Simply put, collective intelligence wins the day when it comes to elevating the human condition and innovating to solve some of our most pressing issues facing societies today. Producing optimal solutions for many of the world's problems that we face today will undoubtedly require a comparative framework to be utilized to draw upon the very best elements from various systems and a humility to acknowledge that our collective existence depends upon information and knowledge sharing practices. The academic community has acquainted itself with framing research within a comparative context and oftentimes powerful, revelatory insights and solutions have been generated as a result. With this:

1. Think of a system, process or way or doing something (i.e. a process of learning or a system of governance) in your personal and professional spaces - do you know another group of people different from you that might appreciate that particular system, process or way of doing something?

___

2. How can you advocate for the incorporation of different practices in your own sphere of influence? What obstacles do you foresee associated with doing this, if any, and who are the champions in your ecosystem to further advocate for these implementations?

**Affirmation**: "I am a solutionist that considers other perspectives in formulating my strategy to solve issues and believes in developing a comparative framework to glean a diversity of insights."

*When we begin to see ourselves as global citizens first, who happen to be from a particular country, we gradually remove our nationalistic desires to, at times, detach ourselves from the plight of our brothers and sisters around the world, wherever they may be.*

The lens through which the majority of individuals from one country view another are largely shaped through limited in-person interactions along with what various forms of media present to us about that particular country. We must remember that the governing bodies and leaders of a country that we usually see in the media are not entirely representative of the people of that country and that our interactions with a minority of people from a country are in no way, shape or form indicative of the mindset and behaviors of everyone in the country. Despite our country differences, we all experience the collective highs and lows of living life, no matter where we find ourselves in the world. The birth of a child, the attainment of an opportunity that will change a family's future trajectory, the loss of a loved one, the experience of economic loss - these milestone experiences along with many others and the range of emotions experienced during these life events do not discriminate based upon the country in which one is located. Think about this:

1. What specific social, political or cultural elements of your country give you the most appreciation as a citizen of that country and why? What specific social, political or cultural elements of your country make you feel ashamed to be a citizen of that country and why?

_____
_____
_____
_____
_____
_____
_____
_____

2. Envision yourself in the shoes of another person from another country or community within your country experiencing an event that was an emotionally high and happy point for you and an event that was a low and traumatic point for you. In envisioning this scenario, is it easy or hard for you to envision and how does it make you feel?

_____
_____
_____
_____
_____
_____
_____
_____
_____
_____
_____
_____
_____
_____
_____
_____

3. How can you reconcile any previously held beliefs or lack of empathy about a country or community through envisioning this scenario?

_____
_____
_____
_____
_____
_____
_____
_____
_____
_____
_____

**Affirmation:** "I am a global citizen first who happens to be from (fill in your country) - I prioritize the well-being of my global brothers and sisters no matter where I am in the world."

*Extensive travel abroad does not guarantee success as a cultural ambassador within another community - there must be concerted efforts within the community one occupies day in and day out to facilitate positive perceptions surrounding the community from which they come.*

Although this is primarily focused on people engaging with communities abroad, it is equally as applicable to engaging with communities within your country that are different from yours as well. As a member of the global collective, you have immense power to shape not only the trajectory of how people from another country or community perceive you, but also collective understanding of the grand diversity of the totality of the human experience. The extent to which you are able to utilize that power, however, to craft a positive narrative of the people from your country or community while engaging with others is primarily predicated upon building trust.

We understand that this trust is ultimately built through genuine, authentic vulnerability with members of a community. Consider:

1. In what ways have you demonstrated vulnerability in your communications and engagements with those outside of your own country and/or immediate community?

_____
_____
_____
_____
_____
_____
_____
_____
_____

2. In those moments of vulnerability, how did the interactions make you feel? Why do you think that you felt those particular emotions and were you at all surprised by how you felt?

_____
_____
_____
_____
_____
_____
_____
_____
_____
_____
_____
_____
_____
_____
_____
_____
_____
_____
_____
_____

3. What elements of other cultures different from yours do you respect and appreciate? How can you cultivate greater kinship with people from another country and/or community through these elements of culture that you appreciate?

**Affirmation**: "I possess the power to actively play an integral role in shaping and transforming any perceptions of my community by others through my speech and behavior."

Made in the USA
Middletown, DE
20 October 2024